Prayers of an
American Wife

Cover Art: www.123rf.com

Author Photo: Victoria Kelly
Cover and text design by Katherine Wintersteen
Titles and text set in Bodoni

Printed on acid-free paper.

Coal Hill Review is an imprint of Autumn House Press, a nonprofit
corporation with the mission of publishing and promoting poetry
and other fine literature.

Coal Hill Review Staff
Editor-in-Chief: Michael Simms
Managing Editor: Caroline Tanski
Assistant Editors: Giuliana Certo, Christine Stroud

PENNSYLVANIA
COUNCIL
ON THE
ARTS

Autumn House Press receives state arts funding support
through a grant from the Pennsylvania Council on the Arts,
a state agency funded by the Commonwealth of Pennsylvania,
and the National Endowment for the Arts, a federal agency.

ISBN: 978-1-932870-83-1 + 90000

Prayers of an
American Wife

**poems by
Victoria Kelly**

Coal Hill Review • Pittsburgh, Pennsylvania

Contents

for Will

When the Men Go Off to War

What happens when they leave
is that the houses fold up like paper dolls,
the children roll up their socks and sweaters
and tuck the dogs into little black suitcases.
Across the street the trees are unrooting,
the mailboxes rising up like dandelion stems,
and eventually we too float off,
the houses tucked neatly inside our purses, and the children
tumbling gleefully after us,
and beneath us the base has disappeared, the rows
of pink houses all the way to the ocean—gone,
and the whole city has slipped off the white earth
like a table being cleared for lunch.

We set up for a few weeks at a time
in places like Estonia or Laos—
places where they still have legends,
where a town of women appearing in the middle of the night
is surprising but not unheard of. The locals come to watch
our strange carnival unpacking in some wheat field
outside Paldiski—we invite them in for coffee,
forgetting for a minute
that some of our own men won't come home again:
and sometimes, a wife or two won't either.
She'll meet someone else, say, and
it's one of those things we don't talk about,
how people fall in and out of love—
and also, what the chaplains are for.

And then, a few days before the planes fly in
we return. We roll out the sidewalks and make the beds,
tether the trees to the yard.
On the airfield, everything is as it should be—
our matte red lipstick, the babies blanketed inside strollers.

Only, our husbands look at us a little sadly,
the way people do when they know
they have changed but don't want to say it.
Instead they say, What have you been doing all this time?
And we say, Oh you know, the dishes,
and they laugh and say,
Thank God some things stay the same.

The Messengers

How can you help
picturing it,
the small huddle on your doorstep—
the commander; the priest who married you;
the women with their sad, drawn faces.
You know
the only message you will get
from the pink, blistered mountains of Kabul
is the one that comes when you're thinking about the dishes
or out buying oranges.
And how can you not see
the faces of these people
in every housewife or postman who pauses
at the edge of your driveway;
even a sack of letters, the dog sniffing in the street
doesn't stop you from sleeping
with the bedside light on.

Almost

I can imagine living a whole life
in the house my parents almost bought in Morris Plains
across from the train station;
the way I almost played Red Light, Green Light
in that park next to the library
and almost went to school
at St. Virgil's Parish, on Speedwell Avenue;
the way my father almost made thirty years
of slow, moonlit walks to the station in winter,
my mother
waving from the kitchen window.
I can imagine growing up,
and almost taking the same train
to some publishing job in the city,
and coming home
to dinner with my parents next door,
to children who, on weekends,
almost hunt for clovers in the same park
I almost knew the name of once.

And how different
that life that barely passed me by
seems now
from this lonely, sunny afternoon at the beach
on some base in Virginia
under the brick-red blaze of summer—
the mothers fortified under hats and sunblock,
the tired children slowing down around me,
and a man
who could almost be my father
waving to the person behind me.

Kwansaba for a Wounded Warrior

Colin laughs and says he hasn't met
his wife yet among the nurses at
Brooke Army Medical Center. "In Kunar, when
we were kicking off, and those hajjis
were flaming up the road, I wished
for any girl. But I'll tell you—
that was the baddest show on earth."

To My Husband, Flying over Afghanistan
A Cento

The pilot alone knows [1]
the chill of closed eyelids [2]
in the glaring white gap: [3]
the wired minefield: [4]
the stars in active orbit. [5]
And all is from wreck, here, there— [6]
the hot black dunes in the air. [7]

Now I am safe in the deep V of a weekday: [8]
how fibrous and incidental it all seems— [9]
the Avon lady trekking door to door [10]
the paper sacks stuffed full of oranges, [11]
obscenely jewel-toned [12]
while the whole cathedral crashes at your back. [13]

[1] Andrew Joron "Spine to Spin, Spoke to Speak"

[2] Marina Tsvetaeva "Poems for Blok, 1" trans. Ilya Kaminsky & Jean Valentine

[3] Medbh McGuckian "Painting by Moonlight"

[4] Ciaran Carson "Let Us Go Then"

[5] Marie Ponsot "Imagining Starry"

[6] Gerard Manley Hopkins "The Times Are Nightfall..."

[7] Henri Cole "Green Shade"

[8] Rachel Zucker "After Baby After Baby"

[9] Sarah Gambito "Holiday"

[10] David Trinidad "9773 Comanche Ave."

[11] Shin Yu Pai "Six Persimmons"

[12] Joyelle McSweeney "A Peacock in Spring"

[13] Kamau Brathwaite "Mesongs"

Standing on the Airfield, Before War

If there is one thing I should say before you go,
it should not be about standing on some driveway in Pensacola,
baptized by airplanes.

It should not be that the house was bare and there
was no food, but we were young and the airplanes
were like tiny glass toys in the sky,
and there was all of it ahead of us then, there was
this whole life.

No, if there is only time in this goodbye
for one last affirmation,
let it not be of that pond blue summer, or letters
from home, or romance at all. Let it be of love when it's
more than this love, when it's not dazzling
or eager or brave—
like an old man before a party,
fixated on a tie, and his wife, waiting
patiently in the kitchen, letting him decide.

The Green Flash

And on certain nights on palm-treed Cayman beaches,
    the renters wander out at sunset among the scattered
chairs, the half-buried sandwich crusts, all the clatter
    of the day gone, the babies glazed with sleep,

and all of us waiting for the sun to move. It's thought
    to sink into the water in a flash of green: we gather around
the few old men who've seen it, the kingfishers hovering
    too, like disciples, aware that more often than not,

you can't look at the sun head-on, like a lot of other things—
    your brother's anxious tics, say, or the war on TV. You wonder
what would change if you saw it, what would happen to you after;
    whether part of you—like the soul of some marooned conch, clinging
to its sea-crusted shell—would suddenly lift off, shudder
    free: rise up with the birds, toward some far empyrean rafter.

The Funeral

On the night of your uncle's funeral, your mother tells you
how the priest drove the wrong way to the cemetery,
while both Aunt Sofia and the hearse turned right instead of left,
and when they finally met at the gravesite, the priest
got out of the car and started yelling at Aunt Sofia,
waving his hands and saying, "Why didn't you follow me,"
because he was embarrassed, and Aunt Sofia cried and said something
in her Hungarian English, and later your father went up to the priest
and told him he should be ashamed, she was a woman
at her husband's funeral—and when it is all over, across the country,
you say the rosary for your uncle at your desk on base
with your work spread out in front of you, and your hands
run over the beads and over the papers but instead of Mary's face
all you can see is the priest, waving his arms in the cemetery,
and your uncle, how he would have laughed if he had been there.

Nights in the Gulf

I wish I knew you there,
a man curled up in a doll's bed and the tailhooks
pounding overhead and always
people up and down the stairs and
never enough hours, never enough quiet to last the night.

I wish I knew you over Kandahar,
the puckered smoke-black mountains
and the gunfire spitting at your tail, and the calls
coming in and going out and in those times,
or when it's over and you're making your way back,
I wonder if you come across angels while you're praying
for the mail, see the faces of your grandparents
sliding past you in the dark.

Sometimes at night,
I walk to the beach where I took that last
photograph of you, remember how you worried
things would be different after so much time, that the dog
perhaps would not know you,
that this life you loved once
would just be one more thing to lose.

Planning

In the bathroom. fingering the wheel of tiny blue pills. you know
that in a month he'll be deployed and gone for eight more after that.
but there is Dubai in August if the flights are cheap. the dripping heat
and those white hotel sheets. and three months later if he comes home
you might be in California. some desert town where they say the hospitals
aren't good and the air is bad for children. but if it isn't California it
will be Texas and either way the sun will be hot and red and the nights
very cold. and you'll be far from your parents who are aging. walking
hesitantly now like toddlers. and either way you'll have to sell the house
by the ocean you came to love so much. the jets roaring in like lions
from the front. and inside every cockpit. somebody's beloved daughter
or somebody's beloved son coming back to life.

On Sundays

On Sundays when I wake alone again
 to the dog's snoring, a day of keeping house,
the bells ringing from the church next door,
 I remember that we pray before different altars—
his a trembling ship at sea, a few lights in the rainy
 darkness, and out there he is not someone's spouse,
not someone's son, but someone far from here, at war.
 At home, things are not the way they were.
Sometimes I dream myself into an old life—
 a game of tag in the driveway, the cats sleeping
in the shade—there was always another hour
 for reading, always my mother laughing on the phone,
and so much time between child and wife,
 so many well-worn prayers, for God to keep me.
But I knew things then I don't know now—
 that God was real, and I would never be alone.

Prayers of an American Wife

Two hours from Santiago by the Pato Piraña bus.
the cookie-makers hawk their dulces on the corner.
They hang their baskets on tree branches: they are tired
as men who stoop over workbenches all day.
In college, I stayed in a hotel over the square.
the sweet smell of manjar curled like a sleeping cat
in the back of every closet—while outside. the vendors
called prices to the children scrambling home for lunch.
I was so far from home.

    One day, three years into a marriage that took my husband
to another far ocean. I would dream back that too-bright place.
Another wives' club dinner. another river-city blackout.
and surely I know it all goes on somewhere still:
those white-eared dogs jumping at the trees:
the schoolgirls sitting cross-legged by the fountain.
teasing and flirting—though I imagine it's possible
the buses have long stopped coming.
the highway petering out one day a few miles from town.
and the black-capped drivers getting out at the end of the line
and scratching their heads. peering into the tall grass
where an old dirt road used to be.

Atlantic City

In the forties my grandmother worshipped
sand as pale as Irish skin, the sirens
of casinos on summer afternoons.
One night, walking home from a dance,
a corsage red as a heart on her wrist,
she heard the footsteps of a man behind her,
    quick and slow, quick and slow.
These were the months of the boardwalk murders,
the curfews and pocketknives slipped into stockings,
but in the end she was saved by a gate—a latch
she knew and he did not—and a sprint to the front door,
while a neighbor's lights came on, yellow
as a cat's eyes in the dark.

In the fifties she married a man who drank
away the scalded bodies of Nagasaki, and
how many nights did she wake then to the rattle
of a latch in the yard, the footsteps
of a man at the edge of her bed,
so her daughter could have a daughter who
loved the ocean too but saw
the wreckage of a different war.

The Departure

Last year my dad dreamed he saw his dead father in the driveway,
leaning against the hood of the red Jaguar they sold in 1966.
Dad thought Grandpa had come for him, but he turned to see my
grandmother bounding down the porch steps, purseless, with her skirt
in her hands. She hadn't run in years. My grandfather held out his
hand, and my father watched as they climbed into the car, waving at
him like a couple of kids after a wedding. Two days later, in the waking
world, my grandmother was taken to the hospital, and the whole time
she was dying she was looking over our shoulders at something in the
corner of the room. It occurred to me that my father, like his father
and mother before him, used to say, Someday when I'm older..., but
then got old, and that everyone who's aged out of our lives might still
be getting older somewhere else, blowing candles and breaking piñatas
and making the crazy plans of people with all the time in the world.

Acknowledgements

Southwest Review: chosen for the *Best American Poetry 2013* | "When the Men Go Off to War"

Alaska Quarterly Review | "The Messengers" and "Almost"

The South Carolina Review | "Kwansaba for a Wounded Warrior"

Nimrod | "To My Husband, Flying over Afghanistan"

The Pedestal | "Standing on the Airfield, Before War"

Barrow Street | "The Green Flash"

Harpur Palate | "The Funeral"

The Hopkins Review | "Nights in the Gulf"

The Chariton Review | "Planning"

Georgetown Review | "Prayers of an American Wife"

Victoria Kelly received her M.F.A. from the Iowa Writers' Workshop. her B.A. Summa Cum Laude in English from Harvard University and her M.Phil. in Creative Writing from Trinity College Dublin. where she was a United States Mitchell Scholar. Her poetry and fiction have appeared in *Alaska Quarterly Review. Southwest Review. Nimrod. The American Poetry Review.* and *Barrow Street.* among others. She lives in Virginia with her husband. a fighter pilot for the U.S. Navy.

The Coal Hill Review Chapbook Series

Co-winner of the 2012
Coal Hill Chapbook Prize
Prayers of an American Wife
Victoria Kelly

Co-winner of the 2012
Coal Hill Chapbook Prize
Rooms of the Living
Paul Martin

A Coal Hill Special Edition
Irish Coffee
Jay Carson

Winner of the 2011
Coal Hill Chapbook Prize
Bathhouse Betty
Matt Terhune

A Coal Hill Special Edition
Crossing Laurel Run
Maxwell King

Winner of the 2010
Coal Hill Chapbook Prize
Shelter
Gigi Marks

Winner of the 2009
Coal Hill Chapbook Prize
Shake It and It Snows
Gailmarie Pahmeier

Winner of the 2008
Coal Hill Chapbook Prize
The Ghetto Exorcist
James Tyner